A  BOOK™

T0011187

WHAT IS MONEY?

BARTERING, CASH, CRYPTOCURRENCY...AND MUCH MORE!

Alicia Green

Children's Press®
An imprint of Scholastic Inc.

Content Consultant
Dr. Marie A. Bussing
Emeriti Faculty, Romain College of Business
University of Southern Indiana

Library of Congress Cataloging-in-Publication Data
Names: Green, Alicia, author.
Title: What is money?: bartering, cash, cryptocurrency . . . and much more! / by Alicia Green.
Description: First edition. | New York, NY: Children's Press, an imprint of Scholastic, Inc., 2024. | Series: A true book: money! | Includes bibliographical references and index. | Audience: Ages 8–10. | Audience: Grades 4–6. | Summary: "A series to build strong financial habits early on in life! How can I make money? What is inflation? What is the difference between a debit card and a credit card? Economics—and more specifically, money—play such a large role in our lives. Yet there are many mysteries and misconceptions surrounding the basic concepts of finance and smart money management. This A True Book series offers students the know-how they'll need to start on the road to financial literacy—a crucial skill for today's world. Interesting information is presented in a fun, friendly way—and in the simplest terms possible—which will enable students to build strong financial habits early on in life. Understanding how society progressed from the barter system to currency—and how that money works in the global economy—are just two critical financial literacy skills that all kids should have. Did you know that the first paper currency appeared more than 1,200 years ago? Or that the currency of the future will likely be digital? Learn all this and more in What Is Money?—a book that starts kids on the road to financial literacy."—Provided by publisher.
Identifiers: LCCN 2022054129 (print) | LCCN 2022054130 (ebook) | ISBN 9781339004877 (library binding) | ISBN 9781339004884 (paperback) | ISBN 9781339004891 (ebk)
Subjects: LCSH: Money—History—Juvenile literature. | Barter—Juvenile literature. | Paper money—Juvenile literature. | Cryptocurrencies—Juvenile literature. | BISAC: JUVENILE NONFICTION / Concepts / Money | JUVENILE NONFICTION / General
Classification: LCC HG221.5 .G727 2023 (print) | LCC HG221.5 (ebook) | DDC 332.4—dc23/eng/20221213
LC record available at https://lccn.loc.gov/2022054129
LC ebook record available at https://lccn.loc.gov/2022054130

10 9 8 7 6 5 4 3 2 1   24 25 26 27 28

Printed in China 62
First edition, 2024

Design by Kathleen Petelinsek
Series produced by Spooky Cheetah Press

Find the Truth!

Everything you are about to read is true *except* for one of the sentences on this page.

Which one is **TRUE**?

T or F   The first metal coins were made in ancient China.

T or F   The $1,000 dollar bill is the largest U.S. bill in circulation.

Find the answers in this book.

What's in This Book?

Ben Franklin's portrait is on the U.S. $100 bill.

Cowrie shells were used as currency for about 4,000 years.

![The BIG Truth]

What Makes Money . . . Money?

4 Money Today

Many Maasai people use cattle as money.

In the United States, every
$1 and $5 bill is used in about
110 transactions yearly.

INTRODUCTION

Money is a part of our everyday lives. It's considered one of the most important human inventions. **But what is money?** If you said it's the coins and bills that people use to buy things, you're right! But money is more than that. **Money is a means of exchange.** It is accepted in exchange for **goods** and **services**. Money also serves as a **measurement of value**. It determines how much something is worth. A very important characteristic of money is that we all agree on its value. For example, everyone agrees that a five-dollar bill is worth five dollars. What we call money today has changed a lot over time. Turn the page to learn more!

Barter comes from the French word barater, which means "to trade."

Long ago, people would meet in the marketplace to trade goods.

The Barter System

Imagine you lived thousands of years ago. There were no stores. There were no coins or paper **currency**. Yet people still had the same basic needs, like food and shelter. People couldn't grow or make everything they needed to survive. They had to get certain things from others. If people didn't have a standard form of exchange, like coins and paper bills, how did they manage? They **bartered**.

Exchanging Goods

When people bartered, they exchanged a good or service that they could provide for one they needed. For example, a fisherman might have caught more fish than he needed. But he didn't have furs to keep him warm in winter. A nearby trapper had plenty of furs, but no fish to eat. Once the fisher and trapper agreed on how many fish could be exchanged for a number of furs, they traded. Bartering was equally beneficial for everyone involved.

Trading toys or baseball cards with a friend is bartering.

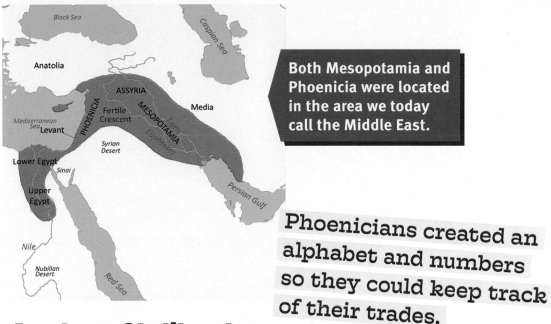

Both Mesopotamia and Phoenicia were located in the area we today call the Middle East.

Phoenicians created an alphabet and numbers so they could keep track of their trades.

Ancient Civilizations

Experts think bartering started in Mesopotamia thousands of years ago. This region in Asia had rich soil for farming, but other resources were rare or nonexistent. Mesopotamians used grains, oils, and fabrics to trade with nearby people for wood, stone, and metals. Phoenicians, who lived nearby along the coast of the Mediterranean Sea, adopted bartering from the Mesopotamians. These skilled navigators then traveled across oceans to trade with people around the world.

Giving a haircut is a type of service. So is repairing a car.

Services for Goods

Sometimes a person didn't have goods to trade. Instead, they offered their services in exchange for goods. Imagine there was a farmer in the village who grew apples—and the fence around his orchard needed repairs. The farmer might give apples to a carpenter in exchange for the carpenter repairing the fence.

Downfalls to Bartering

There were disadvantages to the barter system. To barter, a person would have to find someone with the product they needed. But they also had to have what that other individual wanted. Even when people found good trading partners, more problems could arise. Remember the fisherman and the trapper? Their partnership would end if the trapper decided to trade for meat instead, or when the fisherman had all the furs he needed.

"Sorry. Cash only."

Today, some people use the internet to trade goods and services.

Stores do not accept bartering as a form of payment for goods or services anymore. Why do you think this customer is trying to trade his toad for an ice cream cone?

In ancient times, salt was a very valuable commodity because it was rare and it could be used to preserve food.

Roman soldiers were sometimes paid with salt. *Sal* is the Latin word for *salt*. Roman soldiers' monthly pay was called *salarium*. This word eventually became *salary* in English.

Early Forms of Currency

As time went on, a new way to pay for things was developed: commodity money. This "money" was usually an agricultural product, such as cattle or corn, that people could consume. When used as commodity money, these products were also used to pay for other things. They had value in themselves as well as value in buying goods. The value of a commodity depended on how useful it was and how scarce.

Cattle

Cattle, which included cows, bulls, sheep, camels, and other livestock, were one of the earliest forms of commodity money. From 9000 to 6000 BCE, people used these animals as a medium of exchange. Cattle were a valuable commodity. In addition to being used for food and money, they were used for religious ceremonies.

Cows were a sign of wealth in ancient times. The more you had, the richer you were.

The Maasai people of East Africa use cattle as money today.

When people say they "don't have anything smaller," they usually mean they don't have a $1 or $5 bill. Which challenge of "commodity money" does this cartoon highlight?

The Drawbacks

As with bartering, problems arose with commodity money. People didn't always agree on the value of commodities. Some commodities tended to spoil. So, for example, if a person wasn't ready to use corn right away, they might not accept it as payment. People might also trick someone into accepting a commodity that wasn't as valuable as it first appeared. For example, a person who was offering a barrel of tobacco as payment might hide rotted leaves at the bottom.

Cowries are the shells of sea snails. The snails are mostly found in the Indian and Pacific Oceans.

A cowrie shell can be as short as a grain of rice or as long as a dollar bill.

Cowrie Shells

Cowrie shells were first used as commodity money around 1200 BCE. They were used in different parts of the world, including China, India, and Africa. Most cowries were small and easy to carry around, which made them a convenient currency. They were also durable, which meant they could last a long time. Cowries were one of the longest-used currencies in history.

A stone disk's value can be determined by its size. Larger disks tend to be more valuable.

Some *rai* stones weigh more than a car.

Monumental Money

Yap is a cluster of islands in the Pacific Ocean. For many centuries, the people who live there have used giant stone disks called *rai* as money. When Yapese people exchange *rai*, it stays where it is. These disks are large and heavy, so they are rarely moved, but everyone knows who each *rai* belongs to. *Rai* are like monuments that represent a family's wealth. Today, the people of Yap use the U.S. dollar for day-to-day purchases. But *rai* stones are still important to the island and its people.

Wampum

Indigenous people in North America use wampum for important ceremonies and events. The beads are made from polished shells and strung together to make belts, collars, and necklaces. In the 1600s, when Europeans started settling in North America, they traded with the Indigenous people who lived nearby. When the colonists realized the value that native people place on wampum, they began to use it as commodity money. The colonists used wampum to pay the Indigenous people for food, furs, and other goods.

Wampum comes from the Algonquian word *wampumpeag*. It means "white string of beads."

Here, purple and white wampum were made into a wrist ornament.

Deerskin was a currency in colonial America. A male deer is a buck. That is why dollars are sometimes called "bucks."

Store owners kept track of customers' debts in a book called a ledger.

The American Frontier

In the 1800s, many Americans moved west—beyond the heavily populated areas of the United States. Hard currency, which includes coins and paper notes, existed at the time. But out west, pioneers didn't have a lot of it. Sometimes they used commodities such as tobacco, gunpowder, and nails to pay for goods. Other times, store owners let settlers buy items on **credit**. The purchaser would then pay off the debt a little bit at a time.

Money comes from the word *Moneta*. That's another name for the Roman goddess Juno.

Modern coins are not made of precious metals. They contain nickel, copper, and zinc.

22

The Start of Cash

Around 1000 BCE, people began to realize that not all commodity money worked. They needed money that was easy to transport, long-lasting, and limited. It also needed to be broken down into smaller amounts—like how we can make change for a dollar. Precious metals, including gold and silver, began to be used as money. The metals were still a form of commodity money. But they were the next step toward the **fiat currency** mainly used today, which has no use other than as money.

Lumps of Metal

When metal first began being used as a medium of exchange, it was used in its raw form. People used lumps of copper, gold, silver, and iron to buy things. Gold and silver were especially valuable. A metal's weight usually determined its worth. People also used the lumps of metal to make tools, weapons, and decorations.

Even after coins were invented, miners in the American West used gold dust to pay for things.

Early Chinese societies used miniature metal knives and digging tools called spades as coins.

The Invention of Coins

People in China first started making metal into coins in 1000 BCE. Eventually they developed round metal coins with square holes in the center. This made it easy for people to carry the coins on a string. Then, around 600 BCE, modern coinage was invented in the ancient kingdom of Lydia (where Turkey is today). The coins were round and stamped with images of gods and emperors. Other civilizations adopted the Lydians' coin-making process and developed it further.

社總作合費消色赤立縣水修
印日 元 洞 一空
壹伯文
校 拾

Chinese paper money was made from the bark of the mulberry tree.

The First Paper Money

Paper money is believed to have first appeared in China around 800 CE. Chinese traders traveled long distances. It was much easier to use paper money than to carry around thousands of strings of coins. The paper money was backed by the Chinese government. That means the government supported its use and issued it to people. It wasn't until about 300 years ago, though, that paper money began being widely used around the world.

Coinage Act of 1792

During the Revolutionary War, individual states had the right to issue their own money. When the United States became its own nation, the government wanted a standard form of currency for the whole country. As a result, the U.S. Congress passed the Coinage Act of 1792. Under the Coinage Act, the government had control over coinage and determined a coin's value. The act established the dollar as the nation's currency. It also created a place for coins to be made—the U.S. Mint in Philadelphia, Pennsylvania.

The first dollar used in the United States was a coin, not a paper bill.

The U.S. Mint is a government agency that designs and produces coins for people to spend, save, or collect.

The U.S. Bullion Depository at Fort Knox, Kentucky, stores 147.3 million ounces of U.S. gold reserves.

No one person at Fort Knox knows all the steps required to open the vault.

The Gold Standard

The gold standard is when a nation's money supply is directly tied to gold. Under the gold standard, banks were required to keep a percentage of gold in their vaults based on the amount of currency they issued. The gold standard was at its height from 1871 to 1914. Most countries stopped using it in the 1930s. In the United States, it was abandoned in 1933 in part because people were hoarding gold during the Great Depression.

The Value of Money

Today most countries use fiat money. The value of fiat money is set by a nation's government. There are currently 180 currencies circulating in the world. The value of different currencies is also established through **exchange rates**, which compare the worth of money in different countries. For example, in October 2022, $1.00 U.S. was worth 146.30 yen. The yen is the currency of Japan.

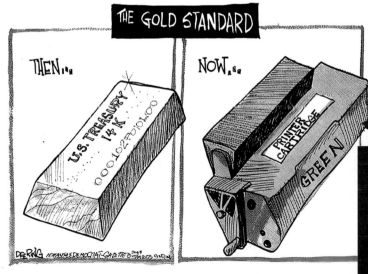

THE GOLD STANDARD

THEN...

NOW...

U.S. TREASURY 14 K
0001023701040

PRINTER CARTRIDGE
GREEN

DERING

The U.S. dollar is the most traded currency in the world.

When the United States used the gold standard, the amount of money the government could print and distribute was limited by the amount of gold in reserve. What is this cartoon saying about the limit on how much money can be printed today?

What Makes Money . . . Money?

Today, countries around the world have their own paper currencies. And they are all unique. Some, like the Bhutanese ngultrum, have colorful and intricate designs. Others, like the Mexican peso, show portraits of important historical figures. But there are certain characteristics that all modern paper bills share.

Bhutanese ngultrum

Mexican peso

They Are Portable

Money is easy to carry and move from place to place. That makes it easy for people to use.

They Are Easily Recognizable

When we see money, we immediately know that it is currency. And we can determine its value by its **denomination**.

We Agree on Their Value

A $100 bill will always be worth one hundred dollars. That stability gives people confidence in saving and spending money.

They Are Durable

Don't be fooled by the name—paper money is not made of paper. In the United States, it is made from a blend of 75 percent linen and 25 percent cotton so that it can last a long time.

SENDING MONEY

SENDING TO
TERMINAL

Amount   17.42 €

AWAITING
CONFIRMATION...

All credit cards and debit cards
are required to be the same size.

Receiving
Mobile Payment

Today, many
people use
their phones to
exchange money.

Money Today

In the United States, money has been made the same way for many years. And it has pretty much looked the same. What has changed is how we use money to pay for things. People certainly continue to use coin and paper currency as a medium of exchange. But we also use **debit cards** and **credit cards**, electronic payments, and more. Our money and the way we interact with it continues to evolve.

Making Paper Money

In some countries, like Canada, the government works with private companies to print paper money, or currency notes. In the United States, a government agency called the Bureau of Engraving and Printing (BEP) does the work. The BEP prints $1, $2, $5, $10, $20, $50, and $100 notes. Banknotes are sent to Federal Reserve banks across the country. These government banks then distribute the money to local banks, where it can be accessed by customers.

There were once $500, $1,000, $5,000, and $10,000 U.S. currency notes

Timeline of U.S. Money

1690
Paper currency is born in the United States.

1785
The United States adopts the dollar sign.

1886
Former First Lady Martha Washington appears on currency. She is the first woman to receive this honor.

Minting Coins

For more than 200 years, any coin used as money in the United States has been made by the U.S. Mint. (The Royal Mint in Wales serves the same function for the United Kingdom.) Once the coins are made, the U.S. Mint sends them to Federal Reserve banks. Then the coins are sent to local banks across the country. The penny, nickel, dime, and quarter are the U.S. Mint's current circulating coins.

The lifespan of a circulating coin is about 30 years.

1996
For the first time in more than 60 years, U.S. currency undergoes a major redesign.

2015
The USCurrency.gov website is launched. It teaches people about the security and design features of paper currency.

2030
Abolitionist Harriet Tubman will be the new face of the $20 bill. Her portrait will replace former president Andrew Jackson's.

Debit and Credit Cards

Today, there are many ways to pay. A debit card is connected to a bank account. When a debit card is used, money is immediately taken out of the account. Credit cards look like debit cards, but they are very different. When a person uses a credit card to buy something, they are borrowing money from the credit card company or bank. Then they will get a bill for their purchase. If they do not pay the bill in full, they will have to pay additional money.

Credit cards and debit cards look alike, but they work differently.

Google Pay and Apple Pay are examples of digital wallets.

Electronic Payments

An electronic payment, or e-payment, is a digital transfer of money. People may make an e-payment when they use their bank account or a credit or debit card to buy something online.

Shoppers can also use a digital wallet to make e-payments in a store. A digital wallet is an application on a smartphone. A person's bank account or debit or credit card information is stored in the wallet. The shopper simply holds their smartphone over the store's payment reader or taps the screen of their phone to complete their purchase.

Bitcoin, which was launched in 2009, is still a fairly new form of currency. What is this cartoon saying about people's feelings toward the currency?

DON'T FEEL BAD. EVEN I DON'T UNDERSTAND ME.

BITCOIN

Cryptocurrency

Cryptocurrency is a form of currency that exists only online. Crypto is used to buy goods and services, but it isn't accepted everywhere the way other common currencies are. And crypto's value isn't determined by any government. Crypto relies on market value. That is the price at which buyers and sellers are willing to do business. People send and transfer cryptocurrency to one another without a bank. They make these exchanges through online accounts or apps. One of the most popular types of cryptocurrencies is Bitcoin.

The Impact of Money

Even before the days of modern money, people figured out ways to exchange goods and services. Over thousands of years, our **monetary** system evolved into what it is today. We get paid money for the work we do. Then, we use it to pay for food, clothing, and shelter, and for entertainment, such as tickets to a fair. Currencies can be used in the form of cash, cards, or digitally. Our relationship with money continues to grow and change every day. But one thing is for certain: Its value in our lives remains the same.

Most people enjoy spending money on fun experiences!

How Do We Pay for Things?

The chart on the next page shows how people in the United States have paid for things at stores over time. Study the chart and answer the questions.

In-Store Type of Payment over Time

Type of Payment	2017	2019	2020	2021
Cash	16%	15%	12%	11%
Debit card	35%	34%	29%	30%
Credit card	40%	39%	38%	40%
Digital wallet	3%	6%	10%	11%

Analyze It!

1 What was the most popular in-store payment form in 2021?

2 How have cash payments changed over time?

3 By what percentage did mobile wallet payments increase from 2017 to 2021?

4 Which payment forms saw the largest decrease from 2017 to 2021?

5 What trends does the data in this chart indicate?

ANSWERS: 1. Credit card; **2.** They have declined; **3.** 8 percentage points; **4.** Both cash and debit card decreased by 5 percentage points; **5.** The use of digital wallets in stores is increasing rapidly, and the use of cash and debit cards is declining rapidly.

Know Your Money

All paper currencies around the world have security features to prevent **counterfeiting**. That includes U.S. paper money. Study the security features of a $20 bill with this activity.

Materials

$20 bill

Magnifying glass

Directions

 Ask an adult for a $20 bill you can examine.

 Use your magnifying glass to find the security features shown here.

Security Thread
On a $20 bill, this thread runs vertically from the top of the bill to the bottom. The thread glows green when held to ultraviolet light.

Microprinting

This will require the magnifying glass! These small printed words appear in a number of places on the bill.

Watermark

A watermark that matches the portrait on the front of the bill can be found here when the bill is held in front of a light. The watermark is visible from both sides.

Texture

Run your finger across the bill—it should feel a little bit rough, thanks to the makeup of the paper and the printing process. You should also be able to see red and blue fibers in the paper.

Color-Shifting Ink

The denomination at the bottom right corner of the bill is printed in color-shifting ink. When you tilt the bill, the ink color changes from copper to green.

True Statistics*

Number of currencies in the world: 180

Number of U.S. paper currency denominations: 7 ($1, $2, $5, $10, $20, $50, $100)

Number of U.S. circulating coin denominations: 4 (1¢, 5¢, 10¢, 25¢)

Dollar value of U.S. currency printed in 2022: $310 billion to $356 billion

Number of times a U.S. dollar can be folded in half backward and forward before tearing: 4,000

Average life span of a U.S. dollar bill: About 7 years

Average life span of a U.S. $50 bill: 12 years

Average life span of a circulating coin: 30 years

Number of cryptocurrency users around the world: About 300 million

Note: These statistics are as of 2022.

Did you find the truth?

T The first metal coins were made in ancient China.

F The $1,000 dollar bill is the largest bill in circulation.

Resources

Other books in this series:

You can also look at:

González, Echo Elise. *What Is Money?* Chicago: World Book, 2022.

Housel, Debra J. *Buy It! History of Money*. Huntington Beach, CA: Teacher Created Materials, 2012.

Roome, Hugh and Anne Ross Roome. *The Global Economy: America and the World*. New York: Scholastic, 2013.

Woolf, Alex. *You Wouldn't Want to Live Without Money!* New York: Franklin Watts, 2016.

Glossary

bartered (BAHR-turd) did business by exchanging products or services rather than by paying for them with money

counterfeiting (KOUN-tur-fih-ting) making a fake copy of something that looks like the real thing

credit (KRED-it) the provision of money, goods, or services with the expectation of future payment

credit cards (KRED-it KAHRDZ) plastic cards used in stores and restaurants and online to purchase products and services on credit

currency (KUR-uhn-see) the form of money used in a country

debit cards (DEB-it KAHRDZ) plastic cards that are connected to a bank account and that can be used to pay for things

denomination (di-nah-muh-NAY-shuhn) value or unit in a system of measurement

exchange rates (eks-CHAYNJ RAYTS) comparisons of the worth of money in different countries

fiat currency (FEE-eht KUR-uhn-see) currency that has no other value besides its function as money

goods (GUDZ) things that are sold or things that someone owns

monetary (MAH-ni-ter-ee) of or having to do with money

services (SUR-vih-sez) a system or way of providing something useful

Index

Page numbers in **bold** indicate illustrations.

About the Author

Alicia Green is a journalist with more than six years of professional experience. During her career, she's written many articles on health and other topics. She currently works as an assistant editor at Scholastic. Her stories reach third to sixth grade students across America. Alicia enjoys writing articles that intrigue children and teach them something new. *What is Money?* is Alicia's first book. She is excited and honored to have this opportunity.